ISBN 1 85854 369 X
© Brimax Books Ltd 1996. All rights reserved.
Published by Brimax Books Ltd, Newmarket,
CB8 7AU, England 1996.
Reprinted 1996.
Printed in France - n°69849-D

Sharing

by Gill Davies
Illustrated by Stephanie Longfoot

BRIMAX • NEWMARKET • ENGLAND

I like to share my things -
Especially with my brother.

We share our toys and games,
And always play with one another.

We often share a bath - and ducks!
All that splashing makes us laugh.

"There's more water on the floor,"
Says Father, "Than is left inside the bath!"

We always share our cookies
When we go outside to play.

But I don't like sharing teddy -
He's rather special in that way.

We share our birthday parties,
We were born on the same day.

So we share the cakes and presents
And the friends who come to play.

When we sit and watch the TV,
We sometimes share a chair.

But if my brother fidgets
I wish he wasn't there.

We share our time with Mother
And sit on both her knees.

We both like playing with Father,
"Now it's my turn, please!"

It is hard to share an ice-cream;
We like to have one each.

But Mother often cuts in half
An apple or a peach.

Things can be a lot more fun
When you're sharing them together -

Jigsaw puzzles, racing cars,
And umbrellas in wet weather.